ROSA PARKS AND THE MONTGOMERY BUS BOYCOTT in Photographs

David Aretha

Enslow Publishers, Inc.
40 Industrial Road
Box 398
Berkeley Heights, NJ 07922
USA

http://www.enslow.com

Library of Congress Cataloging-in-Publication Data

The story of Rosa Parks and the Montgomery Bus Boycott in
photographs / David Aretha.
        p. cm. — (The Story of the Civil Rights Movement in
Photographs)
    Includes index.
    Summary: "Examines the Montgomery Bus Boycott through primary source photographs, including
Rosa Parks' role in the effort, other important leaders, the daily struggles of the boycott, and the end of
segregation on Montgomery's buses"—Provided by publisher.
        ISBN 978-0-7660-4234-6
    1. Montgomery Bus Boycott, Montgomery, Ala., 1955-1956—Pictorial works—Juvenile literature.
2. Parks, Rosa, 1913-2005—Pictorial works—Juvenile literature. 3. African Americans—Civil rights—
Alabama—Montgomery—History—20th century—Pictorial works—Juvenile literature. 4. African
American civil rights workers—Alabama—Montgomery—Biography—Pictorial works—Juvenile
literature . 5. Montgomery (Ala.)—Race relations—Pictorial works—Juvenile literature. 6. Segregation in transportation—Alabama—Montgomery—History—20th century—Pictorial works—Juvenile
literature. I. Title.
        F334.M79N4146 2014
        323.1196'073076147—dc23   2012039242

Future editions:
Paperback ISBN: 978-1-4644-0411-5   Singler-User PDF ISBN: 978-1-4646-1225-1
EPUB ISBN: 978-1-4645-1225-4   Multi-User PDF ISBN: 978-0-7660-5857-6

Printed in the United States of America
112013 Bang Printing, Brainerd, Minn.

10 9 8 7 6 5 4 3 2 1

To Our Readers: We have done our best to make sure all Internet Addresses in this book were active
and appropriate when we went to press. However, the author and the publisher have no control over and
assume no liability for the material available on those Internet sites or on other Web sites they may link to.
Any comments or suggestions can be sent by e-mail to comments@enslow.com or to the address on the
back cover.

♻ Enslow Publishers, Inc., is committed to printing our books on recycled paper. The paper in every book
contains 10% to 30% post-consumer waste (PCW). The cover board on the outside of each book contains
100% PCW. Our goal is to do our part to help young people and the environment too!

Illustration Credits: AP Images, pp. 3, 24–25, 26 (bottom), 32 (top and bottom), 34, 36, 38, 46; AP Images / Gene Herrick, pp. 1, 2, 10, 12, 18, 26 (top), 28, 30–31, 46; AP Images / Harold Valentine, pp. 40, 41;
AP Images / Horace Cort, pp. 8, 14–15, 16–17, 47, back cover; Bettman / Corbis / AP Images, p. 43; Ever-
ett Collection, p. 19; Grey Villet / Time Life Pictures / Getty Images, pp. 22–23; Library of Congress Prints
and Photographs, p. 4; National Archives and Records Administration, pp. 11, 20.

Cover Illustration: AP Images / Gene Herrick (Rosa Parks fingerprinted after arrest).

Table of Contents

COLORED WAITING ROOM

PRIVATE PROPERTY
NO PARKING
Driving through or Turning Around

BINGO TONITE!

Good Housekeeping

True Story
HITLER'S LOVE LIFE REVEALED
BY HIS FORMER MAID

FAITH BALDWIN'S
HAWAII

Cosmopolitan

African Americans wait at a segregated bus station in Durham, North Carolina.

Introduction

In 1943, Rosa Parks entered a city bus in Montgomery, the capital of Alabama. As she paid her fare, bus driver James F. Blake told her to leave the bus and reenter it from the rear door. He said this because she was African American. In Montgomery, black citizens could only sit in the back of the buses. The bus driver was in a bad mood that day. As Parks walked toward the rear door, he sped off. Parks had to walk more than five miles to get home—in the rain.

Jo Ann Robinson had her own bad experience on a Montgomery bus, as she recalled in her book *The Montgomery Bus Boycott and the Women Who Started It*. On the Saturday before Christmas in 1949, this African-American English teacher sat in the fifth row. She didn't know that the row was reserved for white passengers. The angry bus driver got up and approached her. He raised his hand as if to smack her and yelled, "Get up from there. . . . Get up from there!" She ran out of the bus, sobbing.

Parks and Robinson lived in the segregated South. A segregated society means that the dominant racial group separates and mistreats a less-powerful group. In the South, whites had enslaved and mistreated black people from the 1620s until the U.S. government abolished slavery in 1865. From that point until the 1960s, southern whites continued to pass local and state laws that were unfair to black citizens.

In the South, whites created "black codes" and then segregation laws to oppress black people, whom they considered inferior. In the South, whites had their own schools, restaurants, movie theaters, churches, and so on. Blacks were allowed only in "colored" facilities—black schools, swimming pools, outhouses, and more. Many streetcars, railway cars, and buses were segregated within. Whites sat in the nicer sections, typically in the front. Black passengers had to sit in the back.

In 1896, the U.S. Supreme Court ruled that "separate but equal" facilities were acceptable. In the South, facilities were separate but hardly ever equal. White students had decent schools. But black schools were woefully underfunded. Many were drafty one-room shacks. The black teachers earned only a fraction of what white teachers were paid. Most black workers were forced into unskilled jobs and earned low wages. Some still lived on white-owned plantations and picked cotton, like their ancestors had done during slavery.

Southern whites developed various schemes, including violence, to prevent black citizens from voting. White citizens voted for white politicians, who maintained the segregation laws and customs.

As a child in Atlanta, Georgia, Martin Luther King, Jr., experienced segregation in a shoe store. The salesman told his father that he could try on shoes only in the back of the store. King's father, a pastor, left in a huff.

Recalled Martin, Jr., in his book *Stride Toward Freedom*: "I still remember walking down the street beside him as he muttered, 'I don't care how long I have to live with this system, I will never accept it.'" Martin, Jr., wouldn't, either.

By 1955, King, Jr., had become a twenty-six-year-old pastor of a church in Montgomery. Many facilities in Montgomery were still segregated. The segregation practices enforced on the city buses created the greatest discontent in the African-American community.

For many years in this city, African-American bus riders had to do the following at each bus stop: 1) Remain outside until the last white person waiting boarded the bus. 2) Enter and pay their fare. 3) Turn around and step out of the bus. 4) Reenter through the side door "Exit." 5) Seat themselves from the rear forward up to (but not in) the fifth "white" row of seats.

If the five white rows were all filled, new white passengers had the right to sit in the middle rows. This meant that any black passengers sitting there would have to get up and stand or go sit in the back. The bus driver would tell them to leave those seats to make room for the new white passengers.

Gussie Nesbitt remembered being "stuffed in the back of the bus just like cattle," as Robinson recalled in her book. Black riders felt humiliated.

Robinson headed the local Women's Political Council (WPC). Members of that organization tried to end segregation on the buses, or at least improve the conditions. They informed the mayor that the bus drivers (all of whom were white) harassed black riders. Sometimes, they threw the black passengers' change at them. On rainy days, the drivers often didn't let African Americans on the bus. Moreover, bus stops in African-American neighborhoods were few. This meant longer walks for black riders. Back then, buses didn't have air-conditioning. The heat and humidity added to the terrible conditions.

Despite the fact that the bus company depended heavily on African-American riders, segregation continued. More than 20,000 black citizens rode the buses to get to work. However, the bus company hired African Americans only for low-paying jobs, such as janitor or handyman.

By 1955, some lawyers had tried to end segregation laws in the South. According to the U.S. Constitution, the lawyers claimed, such laws were invalid because they deprived African Americans of their basic rights as U.S. citizens. Black attorney Fred Gray and local black activist E. D. Nixon tried to fight Montgomery's bus segregation law in federal (U.S.) court. They hoped that a black citizen would be arrested for violating a bus law so that they could appeal the case in federal court.

In 1955, fifteen-year-old Claudette Colvin and then Mary Louise Smith were arrested in Montgomery for refusing to give up their seats to white passengers. However, Nixon did not appeal the cases. He did not feel Colvin and Smith were sympathetic figures. Colvin was pregnant, and Smith's father was an alcoholic. The black community might not rally to their support. Whites would be critical of the women.

But on December 1, 1955, a woman of fine moral character was arrested on a Montgomery bus for refusing to give her seat to a white man. Her name was Rosa Parks. With Parks, Nixon finally had his case.

In many southern cities, buses were segregated. Whites sat in front, and African Americans had to sit in the back.

Chapter 1

A Fateful BUS RIDE

Parks Takes a Stand

On December 1, 1955, a single incident sparked the Montgomery bus boycott. After working all day as a seamstress, forty-two-year-old Rosa Parks sat in the sixth row of a Montgomery bus. When a white man entered the bus, driver James Blake ordered Parks to get out of her seat so that the man could sit there. She refused.

"Look, woman, I told you I wanted that seat," Blake said, as reported in *The Crisis*. "Are you going to stand up?"

Parks pondered the question. Would she get up? Or would she "stand up" for her rights by remaining seated?

Lieutenant D. H. Lackey takes Rosa Parks's fingerprints in February 1956. This is Parks's second arrest. She was arrested this time for participating in an illegal boycott.

Parks: Arrest Me

For fourteen years, Parks worked for the National Association for the Advancement of Colored People (NAACP). They tried to help black citizens achieve equal rights. They were rarely successful, which frustrated Parks. When bus driver James Blake ordered Parks out of her seat on December 1, she refused.

"I'm tired of being treated like a second-class citizen," she told Blake.

"If you don't stand up, I'm going to have you arrested," Blake said.

She responded, "You can do that."

And he did.

POLICE DEPARTMENT
CITY OF MONTGOMERY

Date 12-1-55   19

Complainant J.F.Blake (wm)

Address 27 No.Lewis St.   Phone No.

Offense Misc.   Reported By Same as above

Address   Phone No.

Date and Time Offense Committed 12-1-55   6:06 pm

Place of Occurrence In Front of Empire Theatre (On Montgomery Street)

Person or Property Attacked

How Attacked

Person Wanted

Value of Property Stolen   Value Recovered

Details of Complaint (list, describe and give value of property stolen)

We received a call upon arrival the bus operator said he had a colored female
sitting in the white section of the bus, and would not move back.
We (Day & Mixon) also saw her.
The bus operator signed a warrant for her. Rosa Parks,(cf) 634 Cleveland Court.
Rosa Parks (cf) was charged with chapter 6 section 11 of the Montgomery City Code.

Warrant #14254

THIS OFFENSE IS DECLARED: Officers F.B. Day
UNFOUNDED   □
CLEARED BY ARREST   □   D.W. Mixon
EXCEPTIONALLY CLEARED □
INACTIVE (NOT CLEARED) □

IOM—PARAGON PRESS—24991   Division Patrol   Time 7:00 pm
                                                          12-1-55

This report states that Parks was arrested at 6:06 P.M. She said later that she wasn't especially tired. "The only tired I was, was tired of giving in," she wrote in *Rosa Parks: My Story*.

E. D. Nixon (left) was a local leader in Montgomery. For years, he tried to help black citizens who had been unfairly treated by whites.

A Courageous Step

E. D. Nixon was a longtime civil rights leader in Montgomery. In the mid-1950s, he wanted to go to court to challenge the city's segregated busing law. To do so, his lawyers needed to represent someone who had been arrested for violating the law. On December 1, 1955, Parks became that person. Nixon asked Parks if she would be willing to file a lawsuit. Her husband, Raymond, told her not to do it.

"Don't do anything to make trouble, Rosa," he urged, as David Halberstam recalled in *The Fifties*. "Don't bring a suit. The whites will kill you."

Rosa ignored her husband's wishes. She understood the risks: Whites would likely threaten her and possibly harm her. However, she felt it was time to take a stand. She agreed to file the lawsuit.

Chapter 2

The One-Day
BOYCOTT

An empty bus rolls through the streets of Montgomery. Prior to the boycott, about three-quarters of the city's bus riders were African American.

Staying Off the Buses

Shortly after Parks's arrest, Jo Ann Robinson and Montgomery's Women's Political Council (WPC) wrote a letter. In it, they urged black citizens to stage a peaceful boycott of the city's buses on Monday, December 5. They made fifty thousand photocopies of the letter, distributing them to schools, factories, and businesses. On Monday, very few black citizens rode the buses. Instead, they walked to work or got a ride from someone else. The one-day boycott was a huge success.

Reverend Martin Luther King, Jr., (standing) was president of the Montgomery Improvement Association (MIA). Here, he speaks to MIA leaders in April 1956.

Let the Boycott Continue

On December 5, 1955, ministers and other black leaders in Montgomery got together. They believed that the one-day boycott should be extended. With a long boycott, the bus company and downtown businesses would lose a lot of money. They felt that if they continued the boycott, city officials would eventually agree to their demands. Those demands included ending segregation on the buses, hiring black drivers, and having white drivers treat passengers courteously.

On December 5, these leaders named their new group the Montgomery Improvement Association (MIA). They voted minister Martin Luther King, Jr., to be the MIA's president. The intelligent, young preacher was about to become famous.

"There Comes a Time . . ."

King gave his first great civil rights speech on the night of December 5, 1955, at the Holt Street Baptist Church. Ecstatic about the successful boycott, thousands of African Americans descended on the church that evening. "You know, my friends," King said, "there comes a time when people get tired of being trampled over by the iron feet of oppression. . . . We are determined here in Montgomery to work and fight until justice runs down like water, and righteousness like a mighty stream." The crowd roared its approval.

LEFT: Martin Luther King, Jr., delivers a rousing speech at the Holt Street Baptist Church. During his speech, the excited crowd stomped on the floor so hard that the church began to shake.

BOTTOM: The MIA held many mass meetings during the boycott, including this one in February 1956. Participants were thrilled that they were winning a fight against segregation.

Pictured is a booklet published by the Montgomery Improvement Association (MIA). The MIA's boycott caused the bus company to lose money. Also, downtown businesses suffered because African Americans stopped taking buses there.

Chapter 3

Walking for JUSTICE

The Crackdown

In December 1955, Montgomery mayor W. A. Gayle tried to end the boycott. He formed a commission of black and white leaders. But they couldn't reach an agreement. As the boycott rolled into January, whites took out their frustrations. Police cracked down on black car-pool drivers. They wrote tickets and arrested drivers for the smallest offenses. On January 26, King himself was arrested for going 30 miles per hour in a 25-mph zone. Throughout his life, King was arrested twenty-nine times in the struggle for justice.

Boycotters walk to work in February 1956. For some, the walk was miles long. Said one elderly walker, "My feets is tired, but my soul is rested."

MOM's Proposal

In February 1956, local black leaders met with white business leaders, known as the Men of Montgomery (MOM). Tired of losing money, MOM members negotiated with the boycotters. They offered to let black passengers use the front doors of the buses. The proposal also said that blacks could sit in the front "white" seats. But they could do so only when "there is no possibility of any additional white passengers boarding the bus." At a mass meeting, boycotters voted to reject MOM's proposal.

Reverend Ralph Abernathy (center) looks at the MOM proposal with attorney Fred Gray (left) and Reverend Robert Graetz (in bow tie). MOM members still wanted to keep the buses segregated.

ABOVE: Ralph Abernathy (center) and Martin Luther King, Jr., (right) were arrested in February 1956 for participating in the bus boycott.

RIGHT: King was arrested in both January and February. Police took this mug shot of him after his second arrest.

7089

Chapter 4

Inspiring the
NATION

Boycotters Arrested

In February 1956, Montgomery's white leaders were trying hard to stop the boycott. That month, a judge asked a grand jury to determine if the boycotters had violated state law. An Alabama law stated that it was illegal for anyone to stage a boycott without a legal or just reason. The grand jury determined that the boycotters were guilty. On February 22, police arrested the boycott's leaders, including Martin Luther King, Jr. Two days later, dozens of other arrested boycotters arrived at the courthouse—with Rosa Parks among them.

E. T. Sinclair (front) was the only black citizen on the eighteen-member grand jury. In the segregated South, few African Americans were chosen to serve on juries. All-white and mostly white juries tended to vote "guilty" for black defendants, even if they were innocent.

Off to Jail With Heads Held High

According to Jo Ann Robinson, the arrested boycotters went to jail without fear. "They were defiant," she wrote in *The Montgomery Bus Boycott and the Women Who Started It*. She added that they were "ready to let Americans and the world know that they could not and would not take any more." These defendants were soon released from jail, and the court set trial dates for them. King's trial would be the first. It would begin on March 19.

In the first two months of 1956, King was arrested two times. He also received hundreds of hate letters, some of which threatened his life. On January 30, a white man tossed a bomb onto King's front porch. It exploded and damaged the house. King's wife, Coretta, and their baby were in the house at the time. Fortunately, they were not harmed.

On March 22, King was found guilty of violating the Alabama boycott law. His supporters cheered their courageous hero. King's proud wife, Coretta, gave him a kiss on the cheek (pictured) outside the courthouse.

"Proud of My Crime"

Though King was found guilty, Judge Eugene Carter was easy on him. He sentenced the preacher to just a $500 fine—not jail—because he had promoted nonviolence. When King left the courthouse, his supporters proclaimed, "Long live the King!" and "No more buses!"

"I was proud of my crime . . . ," he would write in *Stride Toward Freedom*, "the crime of joining my people in a nonviolent protest against injustice."

By this point, King was inspiring people across the nation. Donations for the MIA's taxi service poured in from all over the world. More good news came on April 23. That day, the U.S. Supreme Court declared that bus segregation in South Carolina was illegal. After that ruling, bus companies in more than a dozen southern cities ended segregated seating on their buses. Montgomery was not among them. Segregation continued in that city, as did the boycott.

Montgomery's heroes inspired black residents in Tallahassee, Florida (pictured). They, too, boycotted their city's buses and started a carpool system. Here, a college student signals for a ride.

In Miami, Florida (pictured), bus drivers were allowed to tell black passengers where to sit. But Joseph Sand (left) and Vernon Clark (center) refused to obey such orders.

Chapter 5

Closing in on VICTORY

Boycotts in Other Cities

Across the South, African Americans rejoiced at the success of the Montgomery bus boycott. They began to believe that it was possible to end segregation in their communities. If they could organize themselves and stage peaceful mass protests, they could achieve their goals. In 1956, in Tallahassee, Florida, residents staged a boycott similar to the one in Montgomery. Other boycotts and protests spread throughout the South. These marked the early events of the civil rights movement.

On August 25, 1956, whites bombed the home of Reverend Robert Graetz (left). Graetz was a leader of the MIA.

Triumph in the Courts

On June 4, 1956, the boycotters scored a major victory. A federal court ruled that segregated seating on city buses in Alabama was unconstitutional. That meant it was illegal in the United States. While boycotters rejoiced, the state's lawyers appealed the decision. The case would be decided by the U.S. Supreme Court, but not until November. In the meantime, segregated busing continued in Montgomery and so did the boycott.

Segregationists took out their anger on the black protesters and their supporters. They burned a cross on the lawn of Frank M. Johnson, one of the judges who ruled against segregated busing on June 4. Burning crosses was a tactic often employed by the Ku Klux Klan, a hate group that believed in the supremacy of the white race. Also, white insurance companies canceled the policies of MIA carpool drivers. King, however, came to the rescue. He found an insurance company in England to insure them.

Two members of the Ku Klux Klan walk down a Montgomery street in November 1956. The all-white KKK had been harassing and attacking African Americans for decades.

"We Were Somebody"

On November 13, 1956, the U.S. Supreme Court declared that segregated seating on city buses in Alabama was unconstitutional. The city of Montgomery could not legally require black riders to sit in the back of the bus or walk through the back door. For the first time ever, they could sit wherever they wanted. At a mass meeting that night, MIA leaders trumpeted the news. Those in attendance cheered and cried.

Jo Ann Robinson stated in *Eyes on the Prize*: "We felt that we were somebody. That somebody had listened to us, that we had forced the white man to give what we know [was] our own citizenship. . . . It is a hilarious feeling that just goes all over you, that makes you feel that America is a great country and we're going to do more to make it better."

African-American men sit in the front of a Montgomery bus on December 21, 1956. Beginning that day, segregation on the city's buses was illegal.

Chapter 6

First-Class CITIZENS

Difficult Final Weeks

The Supreme Court finally banned segregation on Montgomery's buses on November 13, 1956. But the ban did not take place right away. Montgomery officials said segregation would continue until they received official orders from the U.S. government. That would take weeks. So, the boycott continued. On top of that, boycotters no longer could rely on the MIA taxis. In mid-November, a judge's decision had banned the taxi service. Many boycotters had no choice but to walk long distances to work.

The Boycott's Last Day

On December 20, U.S. marshals finally delivered the paperwork to Montgomery. City leaders officially recognized that segregation on their buses was illegal. In a mass meeting that night, King told boycotters that they could return to the buses the next day. But he urged them to be peaceful, respectful, and responsible. "Violence must not come from any of us," he said. Nonviolent protest would become a key component of the civil rights movement.

LEFT: Blacks and whites enter the Montgomery buses on the first day they were integrated. After paying the bus driver, African Americans no longer had to exit the front door and enter the rear door. That humiliation was over. They could also sit wherever they wanted.

BOTTOM: Reverend Ralph Abernathy (left) and Martin Luther King, Jr., sat in the front rows. King sat next to a white person (Reverend Glenn Smiley of New York), which had been unheard-of on Montgomery's buses.

An Integrated Ride

After 381 days, the boycott ended on December 21, 1956. Early that morning, African Americans climbed aboard the Montgomery buses and sat where they wished. At around 7 A.M., Martin Luther King, Jr., and his friend Ralph Abernathy boarded a bus together. The driver was polite to them.

"Is this the reverend?" he asked, as reported in the *Montgomery Advertiser*.

"That's right," King said, who took a seat in the third row.

When the two preachers reached their destination, they departed the bus.

"That was a might good ride," Abernathy said.

"It was a great ride," King replied.

The two men had just completed one of the most important civil rights battles in American history. Together, they would fight many more.

Rosa Parks no longer had to feel like a "second-class citizen." For the rest of her life, Parks would be hailed as a civil rights hero. In 1996, she received the Presidential Medal of Freedom.

Conclusion

In Montgomery, white people did not take kindly to the boycotters' victory. On December 23, 1956, just two days after the boycott ended, someone fired a shotgun into Martin Luther King's home. The violence continued for weeks. At a bus stop, several white men beat up a teenage African-American girl. In black neighborhoods, whites shot into buses. Their random bullets hit a pregnant black woman in both legs.

On January 10, 1957, four African-American churches and the homes of reverends Abernathy and Graetz were bombed. Two more bombs went off on January 28. Smoldering dynamite was found on King's front porch. Rosa and Raymond Parks feared that they might be targeted. In August 1957, they moved to Detroit, Michigan.

Fortunately, the January 28 bombings were the last noteworthy acts of violence. Over time, tensions eased on Montgomery's buses. African Americans no longer felt humiliated, resentful, or angry. Many white passengers felt better because there was less tension on the buses. Drivers felt relieved because they no longer were required to enforce segregation. Sometimes, black and white passengers chatted together and got to know one another. In every respect, integration was better than segregation.

After the success in Montgomery, African-American leaders aimed to end segregation in other southern cities. In January 1957, the leaders of the MIA and other protest groups met in Atlanta, Georgia. They formed an organization called the Southern Christian Leadership Conference (SCLC), with King as its president. The SCLC stated that "segregation must end" and that "all Black people should reject segregation absolutely and nonviolently."

In cities where segregation remained, the SCLC held protest campaigns similar to the Montgomery bus boycott. Over the next eight years, the SCLC staged boycotts and marches in such cities as Albany, Georgia; Birmingham, Alabama; and Selma, Alabama. Meanwhile, other civil rights groups fought their own civil rights battles.

On February 1, 1960, four black college students in Greensboro, North Carolina, staged a sit-in at a Woolworth's store. They sat at the "whites only" lunch counter and politely asked for cups of coffee. Though they were refused service, they did not leave the stools until the store closed. News of their courageous act spread quickly. Over the next few years, many more sit-ins were held all over the South.

The civil rights movement was comprised of the SCLC's campaigns, the sit-ins, and other similar events. Together, civil rights activists forced whites to end segregation in buses, restaurants, theaters, libraries, and many other facilities. These courageous "freedom fighters" became real American heroes.

Inspired by the civil rights activists, the U.S. Congress finally supported their efforts. In 1964 and 1965, Congress passed the Civil Rights Act and the Voting Rights Act. To a great degree, these laws finally ended segregation and racial injustice in America. After two hundred years of slavery and a hundred years of segregation, African Americans achieved their dream: to be treated like first-class citizens.

1865–1965: After slavery, African Americans in the South are confined to segregated (separate, inferior) facilities. They are denied other citizenship rights, such as voting.

1954: The U.S. Supreme Court bans segregation in public schools.

1955–56: Martin Luther King, Jr., leads a successful year-long boycott of segregated buses in Montgomery, Alabama.

1957: The National Guard helps black students integrate Central High School in Little Rock, Arkansas.

1960–mid-1960s: Civil rights activists stage hundreds of sit-ins at segregated restaurants, stores, theaters, libraries, and many other establishments.

1961: Activists stage Freedom Rides on segregated buses in the South.

1963: Thousands of African Americans protest segregation in Birmingham, Alabama.

1963: A quarter-million Americans attend the March on Washington for Jobs and Freedom in Washington, D.C.

1964: Activists register black voters in Mississippi during "Freedom Summer."

1964: The U.S. Congress passes the Civil Rights Act. It outlaws segregation and other racial injustice.

1965: African Americans protest voting injustice in Selma, Alabama.

1965: Congress passes the Voting Rights Act, which guarantees voting rights for all Americans.

Further Reading

Books

Bjornlund, Lydia. *Rosa Parks and the Montgomery Bus Boycott.* Detroit: Lucent Books, 2008.

Freedman, Russell. *Freedom Walkers: The Story of the Montgomery Bus Boycott.* New York: Holiday House, 2008.

Marsico, Katie. *The Montgomery Bus Boycott: Milestone of the Civil Rights Movement.* New York: Marshall Cavendish Benchmark, 2012.

McWhorter, Diane. *A Dream of Freedom: The Civil Rights Movement From 1954–1968.* New York: Scholastic, 2004.

Internet Addresses

PBS, *Eyes on the Prize*: The Montgomery Bus Boycott
<http://www.pbs.org/wgbh/amex/eyesontheprize/story/02_bus.html>

The Story of the Montgomery Bus Boycott
<http://www.montgomeryboycott.com/>

Index